AF595675

INTENTION

INTENTION

You Already Know Everyone You Need to Network

,

KATIE REGAN

Ordering Information: Quantity sales and special discounts are available on quantity purchases by corporations, associations, and others.
For details, contact the author at intention@kirkpat.com.

Edited by: Liz Cooper, Lily Capstick, Carlee Jeanne Frank
Cover design by: Mark Pate
Typeset by: Medlar Publishing Solutions Pvt Ltd., India

Printed in the United States of America.

ISBN: 979-8-88797-246-6 (hardcover)
ISBN: 979-8-88797-247-3 (paperback)
ISBN: 979-8-88797-248-0 (ebook)
ISBN: 979-8-88797-249-7 (audio)

Library of Congress Control Number: 2026910869

First edition, June 2026.

CONTENTS

INTENTION

Section 3
Building Your Network

Section 4
Connect with Everyone You Already Know

Section 5
Harnessing Your Network

Section 6
How-to Tactics to Transform into an Expert Networker

Section 7
Setting Yourself up to Succeed

Section 8
Your Next 90 Days

Section 9
Scripts, Templates and Examples

INTRODUCTION

,

"To be successful at anything, the truth is you don't have to be special. You just have to be what most people aren't. Consistent. Determined. And willing to work for it."

Love him or hate him, Tom Brady is right about what it takes to be successful.

Consistency is the secret.

It's that simple.

So, if that's what you've been looking for—the secret to leveraging your professional network—then there it is. Thanks for reading!

But if you're looking for a book that tells you what to actually do (in your life, in real workplaces, with real humans), you're in the right place—if you're determined and willing to work for it.

Networking is simply maintaining relationships with intention.

That's it.

If you're looking for a book that tells you how to work a room, flash a perfect smile, or collect 100 business cards in an hour, this book will annoy you.

If you're looking for specifics, for concrete examples, for guidance on how to leverage your network, welcome.

Because you already know everyone you need.

You just need to know what to do.

You already know more people than you realize.

You're already more connected than you think.

And you're more capable than you give yourself credit for.

Let me be clear: This is a long game.

A human game.

A journey.

My journey started in the kitchen of my parents' house, chatting with their friends.

Today, I'm the founder and CEO of Kirkpatrick Group, a seven-figure communications firm.

The best part? No advertising. No paid promotions. Just decades of thoughtful networking.

Before I ever used networking for something big, I was unknowingly practicing it everywhere.

In kitchens over brownies, homework and dinner.

On soccer fields in between drills.

In hallways after the bell.

In classrooms trying to find a place to sit.

Networking came naturally to me not because I was outgoing, but because I was curious.

I cared.

I remembered things.

I asked questions.

And later in life, those habits turned into opportunities I didn't even realize I had uncovered.

Curiosity leads to lifelong learning.

It cultivates empathy and understanding.

Showing genuine interest in others cultivates comfort and trust.

My curiosity led to intentional networking that led to every job I ever had that led to every piece of new business we generate.

Thoughtful, intentional, consistent connecting.

If you picked up this book because you want to advance your career, switch jobs, leave corporate life, grow a business, land your first job, or generally stop feeling stuck—then you're in the right place.

But let's get some things straight:

Networking is not optional.

- 54% of U.S. workers reported being hired through a personal connection.[1]
- 70% professionals worldwide were hired at a company where they already knew someone.[2]
- Referred job candidates are four to five times more likely to be hired than non-referred candidates.[3]
- On average, salaries are six percent higher if someone lands their job through a referral.[4]
- 100% of my company's new business is earned through thoughtful networking or a referral.

And it's **not just about you**.

Just like friendship, you get what you give.

If you're not willing to invest in others' journeys, you will not master the art of networking.

People can sense phoniness a mile away.

If you think you have nothing to offer, you're wrong.

So wrong.

We all have a unique perspective. Unique experiences.

Even the youngest professionals have something to offer to the most senior executives.

Networking is the skill that helped me build a career I love, grow a successful business and partner with amazing freelancers and clients, all while living a purposeful life.

You don't need to be charismatic to network.

You need to be curious.

You need to care.

And most importantly, you need to be consistent.

You're likely already curious. And you likely already care.

If you're curious about fly fishing, or data, or football, or whiskey, you're curious.

Do not take this for granted.

You can take this same curiosity and turn it into a network that works for you.

This book will show you how.

How to:

- engage with a new connection
- follow up without being needy or icky
- reach out with grace
- ask for help with confidence
- help others with credence
- harness long-term professional relationships
- realize you already know everyone you need

Ready? Buckle up, and let's go.

SECTION 1

THE TRUTH ABOUT NETWORKING

1
What Networking Actually Is

Networking is simply **maintaining professional relationships with intention.**

That's it.

Not glamorous.

Not complex.

Not reserved for extroverts.

You already know everyone you need.

But intention is purposeful.

Like committing to a new diet and exercise routine.

Identify goals.

Set the strategy.

Outline the specific tactics.

Execute.

Intention to help others.

Intention to form and foster real connections that last years, decades and careers.

Connections that people value with you. You mean something to them.

Connections that you cherish.

Genuine, long-term connections.

Real networking looks like:

- congratulating someone on their promotion
- sending a text when someone's parent is sick
- checking in after a big presentation
- introducing two people who should know each other
- following up when you said you would
- sending a quick "good luck" before an interview or presentation
- sending a link to an article you thought they'd enjoy

The small stuff compounds.

The mistake most people make is believing networking requires a big moment: a conference, a fancy dinner, a perfectly written LinkedIn post.

Networking is not an event.

It's not sending 50 LinkedIn connection requests in a day.

It's a rhythm. A steady drumbeat.

With people you already know, and the occasional new person.

Sometimes the drumbeat is loud, and sometimes soft.

Sometimes you can barely hear it, but it's there.

Tap. (Text: Happy Thanksgiving!)

Tap. Tap. (Text: Nice running into you the other day.)

Tap. (Text: How's your dad?)

And sometimes it's really loud.

Drumming. (Text: Hey, do you want to grab a coffee? I want to get your perspective on something.)

Tap.Tap.Tap.

This book will teach you that rhythm.

Because you already know everyone you need.

New connections are great.

But you already have resources at your fingertips.

Tap into it.

"My sister's boyfriend's brother's girlfriend heard from this guy who knows this kid who's going with the girl who saw Ferris pass out at 31 flavors last night."

This classic line from *Ferris Bueller's Day Off* shows how quickly rumors spread.

More importantly, it shows how connected we all are.

I rent a small office space down the road from my house. A woman works in the office down the hall. I can sometimes hear her on calls with clients. She's smart. Kind. I introduced myself to her. Over the years, we've become friendly. Lots of short chitchats. Lots of "Everything good with you?" Recently, she decided to leave her employer to pursue her own consultancy. She asked for my opinion on her messaging. I gave it to her . . . She offered me her services in return, and I said, "No thanks—but maybe in the future." Networking doesn't have to be transactional. It's not quid pro quo. But it is an open door that both of you can walk through at any time.

2
What Networking Definitely Is *Not*

I distinctly remember being in college and everyone telling me, "You need to network."

I also remember no one explaining to me what that meant.

I understood they meant "leverage your connections," but I didn't know how to do it.

How was I supposed to network while I was carrying 18 credits, playing soccer and working at my internship? There was no time.

This misunderstanding, or lack of explanation, still persists to this day.

What they meant was "maintain connections."

Let's call out a few networking myths so we don't drag them through the rest of this book.

Networking is not:

- attending corporate mixers
- collecting business cards
- forcing yourself into conversations
- adding strangers on LinkedIn
- bragging about your work
- pretending you're interested when you're not
- memorizing scripts
- showing up as someone you're not

You don't need to be the loudest person in the room.
You don't need to charm anyone.
You don't need to be a "schmoozer."

Think about the most trusted people in your life.
Why do you trust them?

It's not because:

- they were great at small talk
- they impressed you with their elevator pitch
- they gave you a catchy business card

It's because they showed up.

They remembered details.

They followed through.

They cared.

That's networking.

One of the best pieces of advice my father gave me was during my first internship. He told me that the job wasn't just about me gaining experience that I'd take with me when I left. He urged me to build connections with people in and outside of my department, because I could take that with me, too. Today, I tell our interns the same thing. I encourage them to meet with people on the team, even if they don't work directly together. I connect them with and encourage them to meet with other interns I may know, as well as some of my connections. Experience is great, but so are long-term connections.

3
The Mindset Shift: This Is a "We" Game, Not a "Me" Game

The fastest way to become a great networker is to flip your mindset.

Stop asking:

"How can this person help me?"

Start asking:

"What value can I bring to this person?"

People are drawn to:

- helpers
- connectors

- encouragers
- thoughtful people
- builders
- people who see the bigger picture

Giving doesn't mean exhausting yourself.

Giving means showing up generously within your capacity.

Because when one of us rises, all of us rise.

This is the heart of real networking.

Helping others may not come naturally to you.

That's OK.

You probably do it and don't realize it.

We all have something to offer.

If you feel like you're not inherently a "helper," but you want to be, simply start telling people you want to help, demonstrating that you're a builder.

What is a builder?

A builder is someone who sees value in others and wants to help. A builder shows up, answers, builds, connects. Assume that everyone is a builder until they prove to you otherwise.

"I really want to start helping others with the skills I have. I'm looking for opportunities to . . ."

- serve on a nonprofit board
- mentor a younger employee
- engage and inspire college students interested in [topic]

You'd be surprised that responses could be along the lines of

- "That's great! I know the local YMCA is looking for new board members."
- "I'm so glad to hear that. There is a young man in finance that I think could benefit from your experiences."
- "You should reach out to your alma mater. Most schools love having their alumni come back to speak to classrooms."

Make it a habit.

Can you do just one of these?

Two of these?

Once people in your network know what you're looking to do, it's more likely they'll share opportunities with you.

And once people recognize you as a helper, they're more likely to start reaching out to you directly.

I can't tell you how many resumes I've reviewed and edited over the years. Hundreds (maybe a thousand). And I won't stop. Our babysitter is applying to master's programs. She's smart. A strong writer. Motivated. And she asked me for help with her personal statement and resume. How does doing this for her help me? It doesn't. But I love that she approached me outside of our parent–babysitter relationship to ask for help.

Networking is often in the form of helping others.

And that practice, and eventual habit, of being known as someone open to helping will make you a successful networker.

4
The Art vs. Science Problem

People ask me all the time:

"How do you seem to know everyone?"

"How do you do it?"

"What's the formula?"

"What's the secret?"

And I always want to say:

"I don't have a formula for networking. I have habits." (Cough—consistency.)

You become a great networker
by **doing the small things**
consistently.

Networking is more art than science, but it does have patterns.

Repeatable steps.

Small, efficient habits that add up.

- wishing someone a happy birthday
- remembering a few personal things: spouse's name, neighborhood, travel plans, favorite drink
- connecting two people
- following up
- sending a handwritten note
- sending a text/email if you saw something that reminded you of them

You can't become a great networker by reading theory.

You become a great networker by **doing the small things consistently** and doing them before you need anything from anyone else.

This book gives you the steps.

The art comes from practice.

The first time I realized how networking worked was in college. I had just changed majors from Education to Communications and English Studies. I felt lost, and the uncertainty of my future made me uncomfortable. I had a strong relationship with my advisor Connie who one day said, "You should apply for an internship in the Corporate Communications Department at NOVA." Her neighbor and friend, Greg, wasn't the hiring manager, but he was the vice president of the department. I applied, and I got the job. Years later, I asked my manager why she hired me. She told me it was because of my writing sample. I know that I didn't get the job because I had a connection, but I definitely was considered and provided an interview because of the connection.

In fact, I'm still in touch with Connie and Greg almost twenty years later. After graduation, I stayed in touch with Connie, sharing life updates with her via email once a year or so. I ran into her on the street one day (it turned out she lived in my neighborhood). She invited me over to her house once. We drank rosé in her kitchen, and she showed me all the projects she and her husband Andy had completed in the house. I knew she was an avid runner, so we'd stay in touch on great running routes, also on books we were reading. She wrote a letter of recommendation for me for graduate school. We will go years without seeing each other, but we email once or twice a year. If I'm hiring for an internship, I'll ask if she has any promising students.

Greg was my boss's boss, so I saw him regularly. When I left NOVA, I stayed in touch with him similarly—occasional emails. He invited me to his annual holiday party each year. I would ask about his kids and his deaf dog Winston. He eventually moved with his wife to Canada after their kids were grown. I send him a holiday card each year, and we exchange emails every so often. When I left corporate to run my own company full-time, he sent me a book titled *Soloing* with a kind note. While writing this, I realized I hadn't connected with him in a while, so I shot him a quick email.

5
Saving for a Rainy Day

Think of your network as a money savings account.

Every interaction is a deposit:

- a check-in
- a follow-up
- a thoughtful introduction
- a supportive note
- sending a recommendation
- remembering something important
- a holiday card

Tap.

Most people want to withdraw before they've deposited.

And it feels uncomfortable to ask for help.

That's because there's no money to withdraw yet.

Let's pretend you've been on the job hunt for months.

You meet a woman named Sally for the first time at a neighborhood barbeque and learn that she works at a company you've applied to.

If you ask Sally to put in a good word for you, to refer you to the hiring manager, or to send you open jobs, you're withdrawing from an empty bank account.

That's why you feel guilty, anxious, or awkward asking for help.

When your savings account is full, you don't hesitate.

You have confidence because you've invested.

Using the same example, you could follow up with Sally the next day via LinkedIn. You could connect with a note such as, "Sally, it was great talking with you about [Company] and your job yesterday at the BBQ. Thanks for the great advice! Hope to run into you again."

Deposit.

If you're lucky, you'll run into Sally. If not, you can reach back out to her in a couple months. Something simple like:

- "I saw [Company] announced a new product. How cool! Curious if you were involved in the launch?" Or "Wishing you and your family a happy holiday season!"
- Engage with one of her LinkedIn posts or send a direct message about one of her posts.
- Share an interesting news article or LinkedIn post that you think she'd find relevant or interesting.

Deposit.

After a few more months, you could ask Sally for a virtual or in-person connect.

The crucial part here is that you're clear about what you're asking for, which is just time and perspective.

Nothing else.

"Sally, would you be willing to meet for a coffee or connect virtually? I remember what you said about [insert], and I'd like to ask you a few questions and pick your brain about [insert]. I'd be willing to meet you close to your office or home—whatever is easiest for you. My availability is below. Thank you in advance for considering."

If she's a builder, she'll say yes. Builders aren't afraid to spend 30, 45, or 60 minutes with someone. They're open to the connect, whether it's for a new friendly acquaintance, a good conversation, or free iced green tea.

Pro Tip: Most people can't meet within the next few days.

Send general avails for the next few weeks or even months.

- Tuesday mornings
- lunchtime any day
- any day from 3–5 p.m.

Once you lock in the meeting, be on time.

Heck, be early.

Buy Sally's coffee.

It's $10 and her time and perspective are worth much more than that.

Have questions prepared.

Listen.

Do not ask for anything.

If she offers to review your resume or connect you with someone, great.

But don't ask for it.

Thank her.

Withdrawal.

Then thank her later that day or the next day.

Deposit.

"Thanks so much for your time. I know how busy you must be, so it means a lot that you'd give me an hour. I have a lot to think about on my end, and I look forward to staying in touch. Thank you for offering to review my resume. I've attached it here and appreciate your perspective. No rush!"

And here's the best part: The interest compounds.

Years of small deposits turn into:

- job recommendations
- referrals
- new opportunities
- introductions to decision-makers
- "You should apply for this" moments

These small bank deposits take five minutes each.

Five minutes.

Deposit.

Deposit.

Deposit.

Steady drumbeat of deposits.

Tap.

Tap.

Tap.

Networking allows you to tap into the unlocked potential of the people you know. You earn the help these people might provide you, while helping others around you, and sustaining long-term relationships.

My kids are in elementary school. I talk to teachers, but I don't always know a lot about them, and they don't know a lot about me. One day, a teacher asked where I went to school. Robert Morris University, I said. One teacher perked up, "My son just graduated from there with a degree in communications." My response, "That was my major, too. What's he doing these days?" "Running his own social media consultancy." Interesting. From there, we exchanged information. Within days, her son reached out via text.

- We met for coffee. He met me close to where I live—driving 30 minutes to meet me.

- He was super prepared. Lots of questions. Excited to talk.
- He was patient with me, as I had to bring my two boys to the meeting.
- He sent me a text a few days later, thanking me for my time and insight.
- A few months later, he sent me an email to let me know his new website had launched.
- A few months later, he sent me a holiday card.

Tap.

Tap.

Tap.

Deposit.

Deposit.

Deposit.

And you know what? I have him on my radar all the time. I think about who I can send to him for work my company can't take on or if it's a specialty we don't have. I think about the right time it might be to subcontract work to him.

It hasn't materialized yet, but that's not the point.

His investment has already compounded.

His savings account is growing.

6
But There's Not Enough Time!!!!!

There's a chance at this point in the book you're thinking to yourself:

- This is too much work.
- How am I supposed to do this?
- I'm too busy.
- There's not enough time.
- I can barely keep up with my own family and friends.
- This is too overwhelming.
- I can't do it.
- I'll burn out.

That's normal. It's the same feeling I used to have in college on the day we received the syllabus.

It felt overwhelming.

Daunting.

Impossible.

And then, somehow, I figured it out.

I'll be the first to admit that I don't have enough time to do everything I want to do each day as a CEO, a mom, a daughter, a wife, a friend.

But networking is a priority.

So, I find the time.

And if it's a priority, you'll find the time too.

Because time is a funny thing.

Ever notice how if you have six months to plan a party, it takes six months?

But if you have two weeks, it takes two weeks?

Simple habits, like walking every day or saving $50/month, have real, tangible long-term benefits.

Same as networking.

So, set a realistic goal for yourself, and hold yourself to it.

(See chapter 12 for suggestions on how to get started.)

You can commit to doing one networking task a week. (Spoiler Alert: Section 8 has suggestions on how to build a realistic plan and stick to it.)

Data shows that networking and connections lead to new jobs, better jobs, more sales connections and new opportunities.

Please don't make me repeat the stats from the introduction.

Read them again.

I make it as easy as possible to stay connected. I keep stationery and stamps at my desk. I save people's phone numbers and add notes in their contact card. (Beth likes a hot honey latte.) I add networking tasks to my daily, weekly and monthly to-do lists. Just today I wrote "Send Steve a birthday card" because I got a calendar reminder. This is what I do. It doesn't mean that it will work for you. Try a few different methods—see what works. You'll find your rhythm.

SECTION 2

THE HUMAN SIDE

7
Why People Help Other People

People help because it feels good.

Because it creates belonging.

Because it reinforces identity.

Psychologists have studied this for decades: Helping others increases dopamine, boosts confidence, strengthens community bonds and creates a sense of purpose.

People help when:

- they believe their help will matter
- they feel valued
- they feel appreciated
- they feel connected
- they feel trusted

Reminder: Networking is simply maintaining professional connections.

With intention.

It's not random LinkedIn connections or networking events.

Networking is one way to tap into those human needs.

When you give someone a chance to help you, you're giving them a chance to feel like a good person.

That's powerful.

With nearly twenty years of professional experience, my job can sometimes feel overwhelming, demanding, exhausting. Some weeks can be *hard* and draining. When a young person reaches out to "pick my brain," I can honestly say that it is the highlight of my week. I love that they reached out, that they asked to meet, that they're curious. The meetings themselves are (99 percent of the time) my favorite of a day or week. It's refreshing to hear a young person's perspective and their questions. It feels *good* to give back to the next generation. I feel appreciated and valued.

8
Spotting the "Non-Builders" and Setting Boundaries

Networking isn't for everyone. Some people are in it for themselves, and themselves only. Here are some flags to identify these folks:

- When you meet, they don't ask you any questions about yourself.
- They do not say thank you or follow up.
- When you reach out to them, they don't respond.
- If you ask to meet in a few weeks (vs. right away), they don't follow up.
- They don't do what they say they're going to do.

If someone isn't willing to
meet with you, they're not
worth your time anyway.

Don't take it personally.

It's OK to set boundaries.

They don't respond to a follow-up. OK—move on.

They said they'd send you a link to an open job and didn't. OK—move on.

They don't show up for a planned in-person or virtual connect. OK—move on.

My mentor told me if someone isn't willing to meet with you, they're not worth your time anyway. That really stuck with me.

Pro Tip: If you know someone who is a non-builder, but you can't politely tell them to pound sand, just be honest about your availability. "I'd love to connect, but my workload is unbearable for the next few weeks. I can do fifteen minutes the week of [insert month/ week]. Let me know what works best for you." Fifteen minutes doesn't break your week, and you're still a nice person.

In my late 20s, I received a LinkedIn message from a woman whose name I didn't recognize. She reminded me that she was my intern several

> years ago. I could barely place her. She asked if I would serve as a reference for her, as she was applying for new jobs. I politely said, "I'm happy for you to add my name as a reference, but I must be honest with you. I do not remember our time together at [Company], and I cannot speak to your experience or current skills. And if someone calls me, I will be honest about this." I never heard from her again. She's a non-builder.

What should she have done instead, you may wonder?

She did the right thing by reaching out.

But she asked for something too quickly.

She didn't have enough equity built up.

Rather, she should have said, "I'd love to reconnect. It's been too long. I'd like to hear about what you're doing and what you love about your job. And I'd like to update you on my career and what's next for me."

Honest. Clear.

During that call, we would have caught up on all things work, life, family. She would have told me that she's looking to switch jobs, companies. I probably would have offered to help her—connect her with people I know, review her resume, etc.

After, she should send a thank you note. Email or handwritten. Make sure it's customized to the conversation.

That's three small deposits.

A reconnect LinkedIn message.

A short networking catch-up.

A thank you note.

Tap. Tap. Tap.

If she would have asked me to be a reference for her after that, I probably would have said "I'd love to!"

9
Maslow's Hierarchy (Networking Edition)

You've likely heard about Maslow's hierarchy of needs.

It's a theory by Abraham Maslow that basically says all humans have five layers of "needs." His theory suggests that this is motivation for people's decisions and behavior.

Self-actualization
(reaching your full potential)

Esteem
(respect and confidence)

Love and belonging
(connection to others)

Safety
(protection, physical security, health)

Physical
(food, water, shelter)—
the first and most important

Here's the networking version:

Early-career people		Mid-career people		Senior leaders
• safety • connection • belonging • reassurance • guidance • validation	→	• recognition • esteem • impact • acknowledgment • a path for the future	→	• legacy • influence • contribution

When you understand what people need at their career stage, you understand how to connect with them.

It's a two-way street.

And networking succeeds when you meet people where they are.

As I've mentioned, I love when an early-career person tells me they're impressed by my career and they'd love to pick my brain. It's my easiest meeting of the week. No preparation. No expectations. They ask me what I think and I tell them. I remember being young and asking senior leaders in my field for meetings. I was always surprised when they said yes, but they did. I always did my research and had questions prepared.

As a mid-career leader in this situation, I feel seen. I feel like I'm contributing to these people's futures. And I feel like I am influencing them positively at a time when they're thinking about their next step. In return, they feel connection (she was in my shoes before), belonging (she gets it), guidance and validation of their feelings/experiences.

When I was in the early days of my career, I would ask people for their time. I'd be very honest. "Would you be willing to meet with me for an hour or so? I'd like to discuss my role, my possible career trajectory, as well as how you see our industry changing over the next few years." I remember asking my boss's boss for an "informal meeting" every year to discuss my career. He was a very intimidating man. His office was on the top floor. He walked very fast. He was so smart. But once each year, I gathered the courage to meet with him. I always took a paper and pen to write notes, and I always had questions prepared. I used to think to myself, "I can't believe he gives me an hour of his time." And now I know that he wanted to do it. He wanted to help the next generation. He was investing in me and my future.

10
Being Seen, Heard, Appreciated and Remembered

Networking works because it meets four basic human desires:

1. To Feel Seen

Attention is a gift.

When you remember someone's interest, you make them feel visible. It could be something as small as their dog's name, their son's favorite holiday, or where they grew up.

2. To Feel Heard

Asking thoughtful questions, and listening, is rare. Simple questions can go a long way.

- "What do you like to do when you're not working?"
- "How do you spend your time when you're not lugging children to hockey practice?"

Pro Tip: Add what you learn to this person's contact card.

3. To Feel Appreciated

A "thank you" message goes further than people realize.

Pro Tip: Include something specific in your message. Better yet, send a handwritten note. It's a small gesture that can go a long way.

4. To Feel Remembered

Following up months later tells someone they weren't a transaction.

"I've been thinking a lot about what you said, and . . ."

Networking is simply the practice of giving these experiences consistently.

This week, the topic of graduate school came up. It made me think about Elizabeth, a mid-20s superstar who is interested in earning her MBA but just hasn't pursued it yet. She and I have talked about the pros and cons several times. I immediately picked up my phone and texted her: "Hi! What's the latest on grad school? (Thinking about you and thought I'd reach out.) LMK!" She sent me a four-paragraph response. I don't have any skin in this game, other than being curious about my friend and her future. This small gesture shows I care.

11
Consistency Matters More Than Charisma

The most powerful networkers are not the most charming.

They're just the most consistent.

Great networkers:

- follow up
- check in
- remember
- respond
- keep their word
- show up when others don't

The most powerful networkers
are not the most charming.
They're just the most consistent.

You don't need to be loud.

You need to be reliable.

Reliability builds trust.

Trust builds opportunity.

I joined NOVA as an intern in 2007, was hired full time in 2008, and left in 2009. There were a few people who I stayed in touch with. Some more closely than others. One in particular was Jenn. At the time, she was a marketing communications specialist. She was only a few years older than me, but a decade ahead of me with experience, confidence and know-how. Over the years, we stayed in touch. We'd grab coffee. I'd ask for her advice. After a while, she started asking me for advice, too. "What are you guys doing about [topic]?" "Have you tried [insert new tool], and does it work for you?" We'd talk about people management, influencing executives, and more. I met with Jenn in 2017 after I made the decision to leave corporate. I told her my plans. In 2018, her boss called me. "Jenn told me you're out on your own now, and that you're really good at what you do. Interested in a project?" I took that project, and I have been working with NOVA ever since. My connection with Jenn wasn't self-serving.

I was genuinely interested in her, her work, her life. And she in mine. This curiosity, this consistency created an opportunity 10 years after it began.

SECTION 3

BUILDING YOUR NETWORK

12

Start With Who You Know

Before reaching out to new people, reconnect with the ones already in your world.

Your first connections include:

- classmates
- coworkers
- former coworkers
- professors
- mentors
- neighbors
- parents' friends
- people you've worked closely with
- people you respect

People forget they *already* have a network.

You already have a network.

Now you need to find it. Maintain it.

Find a rhythm. Your rhythm.

Your steady drumbeat.

You don't start from zero.

You start from now.

I graduated from college in 2008. At that time, I felt like I didn't know a lot of people. I bought a two-inch ring binder and added college ruled paper to it. I started listing out people that I knew and how I knew them. Some were high school friends' parents. Some were my parents' friends' kids. Then I started reaching out. "Hi [Name]. Hope all is well with you. I just graduated from Robert Morris University and am working at NOVA. I have so many questions about the workplace, pathing my career and more. Are you free in the next few weeks to connect? I'd love to get your take on things."

13
Build Your Contact List

Keep it simple. Use a spreadsheet or ask any AI tool to keep a log for you.

Columns:

- name
- job/company
- how you know them
- last time you connected
- follow-up date
- notes (kids, city, interests)
- preferred communication (email, text, LinkedIn)

This is your command center.

You're not tracking people like data. You're remembering details like a thoughtful human being. Because we all forget things, whether we like it or not.

Pro Tip: Update this list weekly or monthly. Five minutes is enough. Add it to your calendar. Don't forget. You can add people even if you don't know their last name or have their contact information.

Just today, I ran into Valerie (a woman who is friends with my cousin Steven). I went out of my way to say hi. Our conversation was short—"Hi, how are you? Great to see you. Bye!"—but that's also a small deposit.
A day or so later, I shot her a quick text, "Hi! Nice seeing you. Hope to run into you again soon." Small deposit.

Do not discount short interactions.

These are connections.

People that you know.

14
Add "Future You" People

These are aspirational connections:

- people with your dream job
- leaders you admire
- people doing cool things
- industry experts
- rising stars
- founders
- recruiters
- thinkers

You don't need to contact them yet.

Just list them out.

You're building awareness and intention.

Add to your spreadsheet:

- LinkedIn profile URL
- company URL
- current role
- why they're on this list
- other notes

This list becomes your roadmap.

Pro Tips:

- Make sure everyone on this list is a connection on LinkedIn.
- Notice someone new during a virtual meeting? If they're external, send a LinkedIn invite. "I look forward to working with you." If they're internal, shoot them a message on Teams/Slack and say hello. Then add them on LinkedIn.
- Run into someone from college? High school? Add them on LinkedIn.

Someone on my aspirational list is Maggie Hardy, CEO of Nemacolin and 84 Lumber. I've been trying, unsuccessfully, to meet with her for a few years.

We don't live in the same town, and schedules aren't in our favor. But she's on my list, and—yes—she is a LinkedIn connection.

15
Why Small Details Matter More Than Big Gestures

Most people think networking requires grand gestures.

It doesn't.

People remember:

- the question no one else asked
- the text that arrived on a hard day
- the article you forwarded that aligned with their work
- the small compliment
- the encouragement at exactly the right moment
- the detail you remembered months later

These details say:

"I care. You matter to me."

That's the glue of every great relationship.

Small things compound into trust.

Worried that you don't care?

Well you should be worried.

If you're in this for yourself, reread the introduction. And Chapter 3.

It will be hard to create connections—then opportunity—without some sense of caring.

I work really hard to remember, but I also genuinely care. I add notes to my contacts, and I ask questions to help me remember. Sometimes people will say, "I can't believe you remember that." It's not a badge of honor; it's a small signal of caring.

16
What to Say When You Don't Know What to Say

Haven't talked to someone in a while?

Afraid to reach out to them?

Don't overthink outreach.

Remember the money savings account analogy.

Start with a small tap. A small investment.
This reopens a closed door.

You're not asking for anything. (You better not ask for something!)

You're just saying "Hello! Remember me?"

Try these:

- "Saw something today that reminded me of you."

- "Checking in. It's been a while. How's everything going?"
- "Thinking of you. Anything new?"
- "You crossed my mind, and I wanted to say hello."
- "Congrats on your new role. Looks exciting."
- "Thought of you the other day and wanted to send a quick hello."

Short messages build long relationships.

Simple. Meaningful. And real.

Open the door—and keep it open.

Pro Tip: I love using a person's name in the salutation. Even for a quick email/text.

SECTION 4

CONNECT WITH EVERYONE YOU ALREADY KNOW

17
How to Reconnect After Years

You don't need an explanation.

You don't need an apology.

You don't need a reason.

Use this in a text:

"Hi, it's been a while. I was thinking about you and wanted to reconnect. How are things going for you these days?"

Use this in an email:

"Hi, it's been a while. I was thinking about you and wanted to reconnect. How are things going for you these days? Interested in catching up over coffee or virtually? My avails are below."

People are busy.

Life happens.

This is normal.

I started dating my husband when I was 19. At the time, his sister Danielle was in high school, so when I was visiting his family, she'd always be there with her friends. Danielle's friends and I were acquaintances, not friends. Normal, I'd say. About a decade or so later, I learned that one of her friends was an attorney supporting corporate and celebrity clients. I asked Danielle for her number, and I called her. I said, "Kelly, hey. This is Katie Kirkpatrick, Danielle Regan's sister-in-law." She said, "Of course, I remember you!" I said, "I know we haven't stayed in touch over the years, but would you be open to a coffee the next time you're in town? I'd love to get your perspective on a few things." She obliged. Maybe out of politeness. Maybe out of curiosity. We connected the next time she was in town, within about a year. We talked mostly about our careers, what we wanted to do, what we didn't want to do. A few years later, I called her requesting

> support on contracts—master service agreements, subcontractor agreements, mutually beneficial agreements, etc. And today, she's Kirkpatrick Group's contract General Counsel.

If they don't respond, it's not personal.

Follow up once a few weeks later.

No response? Move on.

Update your spreadsheet.

I can't count how many times I've reached out to someone and they didn't respond. It happens. It hurts. You move on.

18
How to Follow Up Without Being Annoying

People don't respond for many reasons:

- full inbox
- stressful week
- they forgot
- message got buried
- too much travel

Assume good intent.

Try this:

"Hi. Just bumping this up in case it got buried. Would love to reconnect. No rush on timing."

Short. Clear. Human.

Pro Tip: End follow-ups with your availability and gratitude:

"I pasted my availability below. Thanks for your time. Appreciate it."

19
The One Email That Opens Doors

This email works every time:

"Subject: [Your Name] + Quick Question

Hi [Name],

I admire the work you're doing in [area]. Would you be open to a quick chat sometime in the next few weeks? I'd value your perspective and would love to pick your brain on [something]. Happy to meet you at [location] or virtually. My avails are below.

[Insert avails]

Best,
[Name]"

Why it works:

- short
- respectful
- flattering without being cheesy
- clear ask
- low-pressure

Pro Tip: Including your availability makes it easy for busy people to say yes. Let's say that again. **It makes it easy for busy people to say yes.** It also reduces the number of back-and-forth emails.

20
The Art of Making Introductions

Introductions are networking gold.

It's like reading a positive customer review before you make a purchase.

You are getting a first-hand account of who this person is and why you should connect.

No surprises.

Just a genuine connection.

Rules:

1. Ask both people privately first.
2. Keep the intro short.
3. Explain why you're connecting them.
4. Step out.

Example:

"Hi [Name 1] and [Name 2], I was thinking about each of you recently and didn't want to wait another minute before connecting you.

[Name 1], meet [Name 2]. [Pronouns] is/are [insert one to two sentences; be sure to hyperlink to their LinkedIn profile].

[Name 2], meet [Name 1]. [Pronouns] is/are [insert one to two sentences; be sure to hyperlink to their LinkedIn profile].

I'll let you two take it from here."

Clean. Simple. Powerful.

Pro Tip: Introduce generously, but thoughtfully. I like to include something about their professional abilities/ background and something personal.

SECTION 5

HARNESSING YOUR NETWORK

Spoiler Alert: This is where you realize the network you've been building is more powerful than you knew.

21
Networking When You Want Out of Your Job

There's a moment in every career when you think: *I need out. I'm done. This isn't it anymore.*

When that moment arrives, and it will, your network becomes your parachute.

Not the resume you polish at midnight.

Not the job boards you scroll through.

Your network.

Here's what most people do wrong:

They panic.

They get dramatic.

They go quiet.

They isolate.

They think they need a plan before they talk to anyone.

You don't need a perfect plan.

You need a conversation.

Start with five people you trust: people who know your work, understand your values, and won't broadcast your dissatisfaction.

Say this:

"Hey [Name], I'm thinking about what's next for me. No hurry—just thinking. I'm not sure what it looks like yet, but I'd really value your perspective."

That sentence opens doors without alarming anyone.

Your goal isn't a job.

Your goal is **information:** insight, options, perspective, clarity, direction.

In 2017 I was ready to leave corporate and run my side hustle full time. I started meeting with folks in my network who (a) were several years my senior and understood the market landscape, (b) knew me personally and genuinely cared about me,

(c) had proven trust, and (d) had opinions I desperately wanted. I told them my plan and asked for their confidence. I didn't ask for business. I didn't ask for promises. I asked for their advice.

How did these meetings help?

- I gained valuable advice and insights for running a consultancy.
- It opened the door for future touch-points ("I wanted to share an update").
- It provided them information about me that they could share with others.
- It made them feel valued and appreciated.
- I invested in the savings account.

People can't help you if they don't know you need help.

You're not burdening anyone. You're giving them a chance to contribute to your life, your future.

Pro Tip: After you've landed the job, started your company, etc., don't forget about the people who helped you along the way. Send each of them a personalized note, letting them know what

People can't help you if they don't know you need help.

you're doing, and thanking them for their time and perspective. They'll appreciate it (believe me!), and they'll be willing to help you again in the future.

My son's friend's mom works in communications at a media conglomerate. She asked me if I would meet with a young man that she used to work with. He lived in New England and wanted to leave broadcasting to get a job in communications. We met virtually. I connected him with a few people I knew, and I offered to help him in any way that I could: connections, reviewing his resume, etc. And he took me up on this! When applying for a job, he'd let me know and ask if I knew anyone. Eventually, he landed a job. And he sent me an email. Here it is (verbatim):

"Hello Katie!

I hope you had a lovely weekend! I wanted to let you know that I've accepted a position with [Company] as their Communications Manager. I am so excited and appreciate all of the help you were in my job search.

Thank you for everything :) Let's keep in touch!

Talk soon -

Aaron"

That's it. I loved it. First, I know where he landed. Second, I know he appreciated my help. Lastly, he's on my radar for the unforeseeable future.

22
Networking When You Want a Better Job

Wanting "better" is natural.

But "better" is vague.

You can't network effectively for something you can't articulate.

So first: define it.

Better could mean:

- higher pay
- healthier culture
- better leadership
- more growth
- different industry

You can't network effectively for something you can't articulate.

- stronger mission
- even a shorter commute

Once you know what "better" means, share it with people with whom you've cultivated a strong relationship and who want to help.

Say:

"I'm starting to explore different roles with better [pay/leadership/culture/etc.]. If you hear of anything aligned with that, would you keep me in mind?"

People love clarity.

Clarity makes you easy to help.

Pro Tip: Don't rant about your current job. Share your goals, not your grievances.

In 2025, I was catching up with a former colleague by phone. Sarah. We tend to touch base once every year or two. We were both on outdoor walks, talking, and sharing the latest in our work and personal lives. She told me that she was looking for her next step in her career. She shared exactly what she was looking for. She didn't ask me for anything . . . just wanted me to know so that I could keep my ears to the ground. A month later, my company landed a piece of business that I knew she'd be perfect for. She was my first call.

Your network isn't guessing. You're guiding them. They're guiding you.

23
Networking When You Want a Totally Different Job

Switching industries or careers is overwhelming if you try to do it alone.

Good news: You don't have to.

Before you jump, you test.

You talk.

You research through people who are already living the life you think you want.

Say:

"I'm exploring the idea of pivoting into [area]. Could I steal a half hour of your time and ask you a few questions about what your day-to-day looks like?"

People love explaining their world.

They love being helpful.

They love being seen as knowledgeable.

These conversations give you:

- reality checks
- clarity
- hidden paths
- people you can follow up with
- insight into what skills you already have
- insight into what skills you need

I am contacted often by people who think they want to work in communications. I tell them the truth. I'll tell them about the necessary skills and experience. About the market. About the differences between

> agency work and corporate work. I don't hold back. I want them to know so that they can consider it when they make their next decision.

You don't leap blindly.

You gather information until the leap feels like a logical next step.

24
The Kevin Bacon Effect

You are never more than two or three people away from someone who can change your life.

Not because the world is small. But because networks work.

If you want to reach someone . . . a VP, a founder, a CEO, a recruiter, an editor, a university dean . . . you don't need to reach them.

You need to reach the person who can reach them.

That's the Kevin Bacon Effect.[5]

Here's how to use it:

1. Identify who you want to reach.
2. Look at your network for someone *adjacent* to them.

You are never more than two or three people away from someone who can change your life.

3. Ask for a warm introduction.
4. Be specific about why.

"Hi [Name],

Hope all is well with you and the family. I wanted to ask for a small favor.

I see on LinkedIn that you're connected with Jane Smith. I was wondering if you could send an intro message to the two of us. I see that she is [insert title/job] and I'd love to pick her brain about [insert]. Let me know if you think this is possible. Thank you!"

People can't introduce you if they don't know your intention.

Be clear about what you're looking for and what you're looking to do.

If builders can help you—they will!

In 2023, I received an email from Spence, a woman whom I coached 15 years prior, when she was 13 and I was in my early 20s. She was now a middle manager at PWC, and we had stayed loosely in touch over the years. I went to her high school graduation party. She attended my wedding. She said, "Can I ask you a favor? Would you meet with a recent communications graduate I know?" "Of course," I said. "Tell her to email me." This graduate was the daughter of one of Spence's colleagues. She was unsuccessful in her job search, and she wanted to start talking to people in the communications field to learn more. Fast forward, Emma, no longer a recent graduate, has been on my team for two years and counting.

Your dream contact is closer than you think.

I am aware that I'm approaching this entire book from a point of privilege. I grew up in a safe neighborhood and a warm home. With two parents and involved grandparents. My father worked, and my mother ran the household. I went to college on an athletic scholarship. I graduated with minimal debt.

If you don't know people in "high places," this approach still works, because **builders are everywhere.** If you have $150,000 in debt, this approach still works. If you're working a dead-end

Your dream contact
is closer than you think.

job that you hate, this approach still works. If you work remotely or are in a small office; if you're a librarian, teacher, coach; if you're in retail, fast-food, warehouse, transportation, this approach and these tactics can help broaden your lens and your potential "network."

25
Networking as an Entrepreneur (or Future Entrepreneur)

Entrepreneurship runs on relationships.

More than talent.

More than marketing.

More than branding.

A founder without a network is a founder fighting uphill.

To build a business, you need:

- mentors
- connectors

- champions
- early customers
- people who vouch for you
- people who pick up the phone
- people who recommend you without being asked

Your network amplifies your credibility.

I have a vast network, but there are a few people who are my go-tos. My rocks. My stability. My gut-check. They're my unofficial Board of Directors. A small-ish group of people who provide immense value to me as a CEO. The utmost trustworthiness. The "I can say anything" professional friend. The person who will tell you what you don't want to hear, but you know you need to hear it. These people don't even know they're on my board. But they know me. They know me well. We've been in each other's lives for years, decades. They guide me through turbulence or uncertainty. I trust them, and so I listen and take heed. They trust me, so they say what they believe and feel.

If you're new to professional work, this could be your parents, your high school music teacher, or your college advisor. If you've been working for a while, this could be your former boss. If you're a seasoned executive, this could be your peer at another company, the retired VP, or your work spouse (your best friend at work).

Clients are important.

Relationships are essential.

I ran into a guy I knew at an industry event last year. Dan. Our paths had crossed once or twice over the years, but we really didn't know each other. After the event, I asked him for a virtual meeting. Just a "catch up and learn more about what you do these days." He accepted and we learned that we both left our jobs to start our own firms. While we had similar skill sets, our clients were very different, and the way our businesses were structured were very different. We picked each other's brains and vowed to stay in touch. And we did. I asked if he could support one of my clients with SEO strategy, and he gave me the name of someone (Vanessa). Today I work with Vanessa in supporting two separate clients! And Dan and I keep in touch.

Your network is quite possibly the most valuable asset your business will ever have.

26
How to Ask for Something Without Feeling Cringey

Asking feels uncomfortable when:

- you haven't made enough deposits into your savings account
- you feel needy
- you assume people don't want to help
- you sound like you're asking for a favor instead of advice

Shift the script from:

"Can you help me with something?"

to

"I'd value your perspective on something."

People like being smart.

People like being useful.

People like being asked for advice.

Asking for advice is more effective than asking for favors. Every time.

And after the conversation?

Follow up with gratitude.

"Thank you so much. I appreciate your time. It was incredibly helpful."

Those three sentences keep relationships alive.

Pro Tip: Be specific. Call out one or two things you discussed. It's easy to send via text or email.

27
How to Say "No" Without Burning a Bridge

At some point, you'll be the one people come to for help, and you won't always have the bandwidth.

Here's how to say no without damaging the relationship:

"Thank you for thinking of me, and I'd love to connect. Would it be OK if we met in [insert month or timeframe in the future]? Kindly reach out to me then and we can lock something in."

Polite.

Clear.

No guilt.

No excuses.

People respect a boundary when the boundary is respectful.

Did someone politely decline your request to meet?

Here's how you reply:

"Hi [Name],

I totally understand and thank you for responding. I'll reach back out to schedule something in [insert month].

Warm Regards,

[Name]"

Pro Tip: Immediately add a reminder to do this in your phone, in your calendar, in your spreadsheet. Then, actually follow up, and respond to the same email thread.

Pro Tip: Networking isn't always on. Just like training for a marathon or watching your weight, you have a plan that you follow, but sometimes you need to pivot. Sometimes your knee is sore, and you need to take a day off. Sometimes it's Thanksgiving, and you want to eat a second helping of mashed potatoes. It's OK to not have a fast drumbeat 365 days a year. It, however, is essential that you recognize the tempo, and get back on track after a short break.

I love to network, but sometimes I can't. My go-to line is "I want to meet, but I don't have the flexibility right now. Can you reach out in [month]?" This does two things. First, I am honest, responsive and respectful. Second, their response will quickly tell me if they're builders or not. If they respond with "No problem" and reach back out in a few weeks/months, I know they're serious. If they don't, I know they're not builders. Win-win.

Saying no builds trust when you do it well. Respecting a person's boundaries also builds trust and shows respect.

SECTION 6

HOW-TO TACTICS TO TRANSFORM INTO AN EXPERT NETWORKER

These chapters give tactical, real-world solutions to situations every professional faces.

28
How to Drink (or Not Drink) at Events

I know I've said, "You already know everyone you need," but there is value gained at networking events.

But networking events aren't just outside of your organization and labeled as a networking event. Every meeting, every meal, every celebration is a networking opportunity. Think:

- company holiday parties
- company dinners
- client events

Networking events often revolve around alcohol.

Here's the rule:

Stay sharp. Always.

If you drink:

- keep it to one
- sip slowly
- hydrate
- know your limits

If you don't drink:

- order sparkling water or club soda with lime. It looks the same. Also, no one cares.

Professionals respect clarity.

Clients trust composure.

Here are several responses when someone says, "Why aren't you drinking?"

- "I have to drive tonight."
- "I prefer club soda."
- "I just don't feel like it."
- "I'm not drinking tonight."
- "I have an important meeting in the morning."

The point of any event is connection, not cocktails.

29
How to Get Off a Bad Networking Call

Not every conversation clicks.

Some calls drag. Some feel off. Some just aren't useful.

This exit strategy is polite and simple:

"Thank you so much for your time. This was helpful. I'll let you get back to your day."

Short. Respectful. Appreciative.

You end the call without awkwardness.

Pro Tip: If you realize you misaligned expectations, follow up with:

"I appreciate the time today. Thank you again."

No bridges burned.

No weird energy.

30
How to End a Networking Call/Meeting Early (Gracefully)

Sometimes a meeting finishes early.

Sometimes a conversation hits a natural end.

Don't drag it out.

Say:

"Looks like we covered everything. I'll let you get back to your day. Thank you so much for your time."

This does two things:

- signals respect for their time
- leaves them with a positive impression

31
How to Handle Cold Connects

Cold outreach works . . . when it's human.

Use this structure:

Subject: Hello and Quick Question

Message:

"Hi [Name],

My name is [Name], and I really admire the work you're doing in [area]. I'm exploring [topic] and am reaching out to see if you'd be open to a short conversation. I'd love to get your perspective. I pasted my availabilities below. Let me know if a 15–30 min slot works for you, and I'll send a calendar invite. Thanks so much.

[insert days, times]

Best,

[Name]"

Warm. Respectful. Authentic.

No one wants an essay.

No one wants a pitch.

People respond to sincerity.

I love a cold call email that tells me what I need to know and gives me a clear action. What do you want? Fifteen minutes of my time. When are you free? I see options. I don't want to send six emails before talking to you. Keep it simple and clear.

Here's an example of cold call emails or LinkedIn InMail I loathe. "Hi Katie, I find your background to be really interesting, and I'd love to find ways that we can bring value to each other. I look forward to hearing from you." I don't know what you want, and I don't know when you're free.

32
What to Do When You Forget Someone's Name

I hate when this happens.

Forgetting names is universal.

It happens to brilliant people every day.

The fix is simple:

"Hi. I know we've met, but your name just escaped me. Remind me?"

"Hi. I'm Katie. I know you, but I can't remember your name."

People appreciate honesty.

Pretending is worse than admitting.

A woman approached me in a grocery store and said, "I love your jeans. Where did you get them?" I told her. A few weeks later, I ran into her at the soccer fields. We introduced ourselves properly. I saw her again a few weeks later. I forgot her name. "Hey, pants girl," she said. I said, "Hey, pants." This went on for months, until one day, I said, "Pants, I am so sorry, I know I should know this, but I have no idea what your actual name is." "Me too!" she said. The best part about this interaction is that she's now one of my favorite friends. In addition, her husband is also a small business owner with clients in the oil and gas industry. While our clients are very different, our business model is very similar. I call him from time to time to ask for his advice, and he does the same to me.

33
How to Network Through Someone Else's Network

One of the most underutilized networking tools is a simple question:

"Do you know anyone else I should talk to?"

This does three things:

1. Expands your network instantly
2. Makes the other person feel wise
3. Opens doors you didn't know existed

People love recommending people they like.

Pro Tip: When someone gives you a name, follow up quickly, and thank the referrer with a personalized note.

The summer after I left corporate America, I reached out to a former colleague to see if he wanted to catch up. My family and I were going to Deep Creek Lake, Maryland, for a weekend, and I knew he and his family spent time there. He invited us out on his boat for an afternoon. He, his wife, my husband and I were talking about my business and plans. He said, "What's your next big hurdle? What do you need?" I said, "I need really good people who can do things I can't." He asked, "Like what?" I said, "Graphic design, for one." He and his wife smiled. She said, "I'm a graphic designer." She was a former marketing agency account manager and graphic designer (among other things) and stepped away from full-time work when their kids were little and they started moving around. She did freelance work and was open to collaborating. She and I met for coffee a few weeks later, and we've been working on projects together since (seven years and counting).

34
How to Follow Up After Any Interaction

This single technique elevates your networking more than anything else.

After a meeting, call, or conversation, send:

"Great talking today. I appreciated your insight about [insert]. Some of my favorite takeaways are:

- [key point 1]
- [key point 2]

Thanks again. Looking forward to staying in touch."

This message anchors the interaction.

It reinforces your presence.

It shows you were listening.

Tap.

Most people don't do this.

You should.

35
How to Tell If It's Just Not Working

Not every relationship will evolve—and that's okay.

Ask yourself:

- Am I giving consistently?
- Am I following up?
- Am I showing genuine interest?
- Have I been clear about my goals?
- Are they a builder or not?

If yes, and it's still not connecting, it's not personal. It's chemistry. Or they're not a builder.

Move on.

Your network doesn't need
to be huge.
It needs to be healthy.

Your network doesn't need to be huge.

It needs to be healthy.

SECTION 7

SETTING YOURSELF UP TO SUCCEED

So you're ready to leave your current employer, or you just graduated, or you want to get out of retail, or you want to start your own business.

Regardless of how many years of experience you have, you're looking for a change.

In order for your network to work for you, you need to work for you.

Because the whole point is that you want to take the step, make the jump, land the job.

There is a goal.

And in order to achieve your goal, you need to be ready.

So, let's get you ready.

36
Should You Bring Your Whole Self to Work?

Should you "bring your whole self to work?"

It's an ongoing debate, a concept that I've gone back and forth on.

And I've landed on "Bring your authentic self to work, but read the room."

You can be authentically yourself, and still be professional.

Because your personal brand is what people say about you when you're not there.

Whether or not you want one, you have one.

It's what people say about you when you're not in the room.

And it determines whether or not your genuine connection will recommend you for a job, or connect you to someone else.

Your personal brand is built from:

- how you treat people
- how reliable you are
- how you communicate
- how you respond under pressure
- your tone
- your follow-through
- your presence
- your work

Think about one of your favorite brands.

Why do you like it?

What makes it great?

Volvo cars are known for safety.

Rolex watches are known for quality.

Duke is known for basketball (among other things).

Montblanc has amazing pens.

Adidas makes soccer shoes.

Whatever! My point is consumer brands exist, and so do personal brands. And what you do and how you manage your brand matters.

What do you think people say about you? Jot down three to five things.

____

____

____

I have a vivid memory of being in a leadership team meeting at my former employment. We were discussing leader succession plans and top talent within the organization. Literally, faces and names up on a huge projection screen, and we were talking openly and honestly about people, their performance and their leadership potential. One leader brought up a woman's name. Let's call her Clara. They explained how smart Clara was, how great Clara's results were, and how she should be considered for leadership roles. However, several other leaders brought up Clara's "inappropriate behavior" within the workplace. She cursed too much. She gossiped. She told not-safe-for-work (NSFW) jokes and stories. At the end of the day, her name was removed from the top talent list because "she wasn't leadership material."

Now, whether or not this was right, it was reality. She was known for her skills and capability. And she was known for being what leaders deemed inappropriate. And they saw it as a liability with customers and her direct reports.

OK, don't be scared or intimidated.

It's never too late to rebrand or start branding.

And you don't need a fancy statement.

You need clarity.

Write down your best traits: the traits people consistently observe in you. Consider asking your allies what they say about you when you're not in the room. Your allies are trusted peers, your mentor, your former coworker, your siblings.

Early in my career, I didn't think about my personal brand. I worked hard, but I was also trying really hard to be funny and interesting. I wanted people to like me. One day, my dad said to me, "Don't take this the wrong way, but sometimes your light personality can come off as flakiness or aloofness. Don't change who you are, but I want you to think about how people talk about you when you're not there. When a new opportunity comes up, will they want to hire the funny girl with brown hair on the second floor? Or Katie, that whip-smart intern who has tons of potential?"

I didn't change much, but I became more self-aware.

Was I at lunch with a friendly coworker, or was I in a meeting?

When I saw a VP in the elevator, did I tell an awkward joke, or did I say something about a project I was working on?

Your brand matters.

And you can start building it now.

Stay true to who you are, but read the room.

37
Be Who You Want to Be (On Purpose)

Think of someone you admire professionally.

Why do you admire them?

____

____

____

Common answers:

- they make people feel comfortable
- they command a room
- they're consistently thoughtful
- they're calm under pressure

- they're reliable
- they're generous
- they're impressive without trying

You're not copying them. You're naming the qualities you want to embody, emulate.

Now choose three to five traits you want to be known for.

____

____

____

Now ask:
"What actions support these traits?"
"What behaviors sabotage them?"

____

____

____

This is where brand becomes practice.

Live these traits every day. Build them into your personal brand.

What does a personal brand have to do with networking, Katie?!

It matters because you can network like crazy, you can do everything this book tells you to do, but if you aren't someone with a positive reputation, someone who embodies some of the traits above, then people won't connect you.

They won't recommend you.

They won't stick their neck out for you.

They may tell a hiring manager, "He's super smart, but he's kind of a d*ck."

"She's super qualified, but she isn't great at working within teams."

I want you to think about these traits with every meeting, every LinkedIn post, every elevator pitch.

You don't have to be a saint. You don't have to be perfect.

But you should be intentional and consistent about building your brand.

When I was in my mid-20s, I wanted people to think I was good at my job, that I was hungry to learn, and that I could be trusted. My personal brand was:

- hardworking and reliable
- willing to learn, and learns fast
- trustworthy

In my 30s, my personal brand was

- someone you want in the room when making tough decisions
- someone you reach out to for guidance, someone you can trust
- strong people leader

Here are mine today:

- confident without arrogance
- professional but approachable
- straight-shooting, honest and reliable

When I was rebranding my company in 2022, I hired Luke, a brand architect. We were working on the brand of the company, but ultimately, we concluded that I was the brand of the company. He helped me figure out my personal brand traits through a series of exercises (two half-day sessions). Today, Kirkpatrick Group's brand architecture is the north star of who we are and how we work.

Now it's your turn.

Once you identify the three to five traits you want to be known for, share them with a few people you can trust. Your boss. Your mentor. A trusted peer.

Ask for feedback. If they say, "I wouldn't say these are you," ask them what you can do differently to embody these traits.

Then do it.

____

____

____

38
Build Your Elevator Pitch

❟

Here's the trick:

Your elevator pitch is not a commercial.

It's not a monologue.

It's not a TED talk.

You don't always have time for a 10-minute explanation.

You need to make an impact. And you have about 20 to 30 seconds to do it.

It's simply:

- who you are
- what you do
- what you want
- said confidently and briefly

Example for when you meet someone randomly:

"I help companies and brands tell their stories. I'm exploring opportunities in corporate communications and brand strategy."

Example for when you meet someone new in your company (cough—like an executive):

"I am a [title or occupation], and I'm on the [department] team. I'm responsible for [insert]. Most recently I worked on [insert]."

Short. Clear. Human. Memorable.

A person of influence will walk away with a strong impression of you and how you were clear about who you are.

Instead of walking away and forgetting about you immediately.

I had an elevator pitch from the time I was an intern. I'd practice it when I was driving to work. Here's an example of how it went: "My name is Katie Kirkpatrick, and I'm an intern in the corporate communications department. I support internal and external communications. Anything from writing intranet stories to drafting news releases. When I'm not working, I attend Robert Morris University and play on the women's soccer team."

Easy. Real. Short.

I remember talking to the head of HR while washing my hands in the bathroom. It wasn't much. Maybe a two-minute conversation. But later that week, my boss's boss said, "Hey, the head of HR told me she met you. She said you seem like a bright kid and that we're lucky to have you on the team." A memorable impression, because I was ready to talk to her.

Later in my career it sounded like, "I am director of communications. I lead internal and external comms strategy and execution for the residential paint division, including our 7,500 employees and all brand PR. Most recently, we secured about 750,000 impressions for the latest product launch."

Today my elevator pitch is, "I founded and run a boutique communications and PR firm, supporting brands and companies in the industrial space. From Fortune 500 companies to nonprofits, we help organizations tell their stories to the people they want to reach most."

Pro Tip: After I meet someone, I usually find them on LinkedIn and ask them to connect. "Great running into you at the event in Pittsburgh last night. Hope our paths find a way to cross again."

Tap.

What kind of impression do you want to make?

Will they remember you?

How will they feel after you meet them?

____

____

____

39
Have Your Tools Ready

Before you start intentionally reaching out to enhance your connections, clean up your foundation.

Think of this as housekeeping for your professional life. (You don't want to run into your ex in your pajamas without your hair combed, do you?)

Resume

Keep this up to date.

When I was early in my career, I updated it once a quarter.

It was always ready to share.

I never wanted to be in a position where someone of influence said, "Send me your resume," and it took a week for me to update it and send it.

Pro Tip: Send your resume to two to three brutally honest friends. Tell them not to be nice. Instead, be useful.

Social Media

My opinion is that LinkedIn is the only social media channel that matters for professional networking. Everything else is personal.

Check your Instagram, TikTok, Facebook, X, etc.

Ask yourself:
"Would I want a future boss to see this?"

If the answer is no, address it.

If you want to say personal things, and share political opinions, and complain about your kids, and share funny memes, that's fine. Make these profiles private.

Because when a hiring manager or HR rep searches you (and they will), what do you want them to find? Pictures of you in college holding a Bud Light with one eye half open?

Your social media profiles should say:
"This is someone I want to work with."
Not, "Wow, they're unhinged."

LinkedIn

There are a plethora of books written about how to use LinkedIn. This is not one of those books.

What you need to know is that your profile is often a first impression.

A few rules:

- Your photo should look like you today.
- Your headline should say what you do, not a vague slogan.
- Your About section should sound like a human.
- Your Experience section should be clear and skimmable.

On LinkedIn, activity matters. Lurking without engaging doesn't build relationships.

Activity is:

- commenting on someone's post
- sharing an interesting post with your own thoughts
- giving a "thumbs up" to a post

LinkedIn isn't your diary.

It's a lobby for your personal brand.

Build your activity into your rhythm.

Don't have a LinkedIn account? That's OK, too, but it is harder for people to find you and for you to connect with them.

Consider some type of online presence—a simple website (www.yournamehere.com). Something so that when the HR manager searches your name, something accurate shows up.

Your Email

I can't tell you how many times I've reviewed a resume and passed over it because of their email. I love cats, but catlady912@yahoo.com? BrahLife2007@gmail.com? C'mon!

You need a professional email.

Not your old college one.

Not a joke.

Not anything that references sports or inside jokes.

Then, add a professional signature.

Turn on notifications.

Respond in a reasonable timeframe.

SECTION 8

YOUR NEXT 90 DAYS

40
Your Networking Plan (Beginner Version)

If you're brand new to networking—or if you feel stuck—start small.

The next 90 days are about getting comfortable with consistency.

Week 1: Build Your List

Spend 20 minutes creating your contact list.

Don't overthink it.

Just write down everyone you know professionally.

If you've never had a job, write down names of people you know, like your friends' parents.

Early in my career, I didn't worry about gaining anything. I just wanted to know people. Some of these relationships didn't yield professional results for 15 years. This is a marathon, not a sprint.

Week 2: Refresh Your Foundation

Update your:

- resume
- LinkedIn
- email signature
- social presence

This is your professional hygiene.

Week 3: Reconnect With Five People

Send five simple messages:

"Hi. Thinking of you. How are you?"

That's it. You're opening the door.

Week 4: Add 10 "Future You" Contacts

Identify people with the job or career you want.

Add them to your list.

That's your first month.

Nothing wild. Just steady movement.

Pro Tip: If you meet someone new at your company or another company, connect with them on LinkedIn within one to two days while it's still fresh in their memory. Add a short note that says you look forward to working with them or that it was nice to meet them.

Pro Tip: Find someone in a different department who seems to be around your age/experience-level. Ask them to coffee or lunch. Say, "I really don't know much about [insert], but I'd love to learn more. Would you be open to a coffee? I have so many questions, and I'd be happy to answer any questions you may have about our [insert] work."

41
Your Networking Plan (Level-Up Version)

This plan is for people who already have a network but want to strengthen it.

Month 1: Two Conversations

Coffee or video—your choice.

Reach out to two people you haven't talked to in months.

Use: "Would you be open to catching up sometime this month?"

Month 2: Three Introductions

Between colleagues.

Between friends.

Between industries.

Introduce three people in your network who should know each other.

This builds massive goodwill.

Pro Tip: Make introductions a habit. At this point in your networking journey, it should be once every two months, minimum.

Month 3: One Brave Reach-Out Per Month

Remember that Future You list of people you created?

Reach out to someone who intimidates you (in a good way).

Someone you admire.

Someone whose traits you want to emulate.

Someone a few steps ahead.

Someone doing the work you want to do.

Send the "Quick Question" email from earlier chapters.

Pro Tip: Work from the lobby of a busy hotel in your city every few months. You'd be surprised how many people you know walk through there on any given day. It's an opportunity for a quick hello and a "so great to see you" conversation.

42
Your Networking Plan (Advanced Version)

This is for readers who want to maximize the power of their long-term relationships.

Step 1: Tell Your Trusted People Your Goals

You need clarity and visibility.

During a virtual or in-person networking meeting say: "I'm exploring [insert] next year. If you hear of anything aligned with that, I'd love to be considered."

Step 2: Host a Small Networking Lunch

Pick four to six people from different corners of your work life. Could be people from different departments, or people from different companies who all work in similar departments.

Bring them together without an agenda. "Let's get together for lunch."

Your network doesn't need to be siloed.

You're the connector.

"I brought us all together because I think we have a lot in common. I wanted different parts of my world to collide."

The vibe should be laid back.

No expectations.

No rules.

After the lunch (same day or later in the week), send a text or email with everyone on it.

"Great catching up with everyone. Sharing contact information. Let's do it again soon."

Breaking bread with folks is a great way to get to know them. You know what they like to eat, what they like to drink, if they have a dietary restriction. You know if they arrive early or late. And it's an opportunity to ask them something more personal than you might in the office or during a virtual meeting.

Early in my career, I didn't want to go to lunch with anyone. I just wanted to work. I did eventually start having lunch with people in different departments, and it really helped expand my internal network. It helped me when I had a question about finance or logistics—I could ask people from other functions questions without feeling dumb. And when I left that company, I held on to those connections.

My family and I moved from Pennsylvania to West Virginia in 2022, and I didn't know anyone. Shortly after the move, Luke, a former colleague, invited me to his son's first birthday party. While there, he said, "You have to meet someone." It was a coworker and friend of his who had also moved to West Virginia and lived in my city! She worked in marketing, had young kids, and knew few people in the town. We chatted and exchanged information. A few weeks later she invited me out to lunch with some friends.

All working moms. All different areas of expertise: finance, law, operations. One woman's children went to the same school as my children. To this day, we all get together from time to time. Has this yielded results professionally for me? Not really. But the woman who works in finance connected me with her company's head of marketing. And the operations woman connected me with her company's head of communications. And most importantly I made friends in a city where I had none. And I have a group of smart women I can reach out to when I need a different perspective. Or a giggle.

Step 3: Make Five Cross-Industry Introductions

Cross-industry conversations ignite curiosity. People love unexpected connections.

You also learn something new and different. It expands your thinking and knowledge.

Step 4: Follow Up Like a Pro

After each interaction, send one message within a day or two:

"Thanks again. I really valued your insight about [insert insight here]."

This habit alone will make you more memorable and a better networker.

43
Your 10-Day Confidence Kickstart

This is your fast-start plan, something you can use anytime your network needs a boost.

- **Day 1:** Update your LinkedIn About section.
- **Day 2:** Compliment someone on recent work.
- **Day 3:** Reconnect with one old contact.
- **Day 4:** Send a gratitude email.
- **Day 5:** Add five Future You contacts.
- **Day 6:** Comment thoughtfully on someone's LinkedIn post.
- **Day 7:** Ask a mentor one question.
- **Day 8:** Make one introduction.

- **Day 9:** Reach out to someone you admire.
- **Day 10:** Schedule a coffee or video chat.

Ten days.

Ten small moves.

A huge confidence shift.

44
A Simple Weekly Networking Routine

Pick one of these—not all.

Simplicity works.

Option 1: Monday Morning Message

Start your week by reaching out to one person.

Keeps you connected.

Option 2: Wednesday Coffee

One weekly conversation—virtual or in person.

Builds momentum.

Consistency builds reputation.

Reputation builds opportunity.

Option 3: Friday Gratitude Note

End your week with a thank-you.

Closes the loop on relationships.

Consistency builds reputation.

Reputation builds opportunity.

It's easy to forget or to skip these important tasks.

"Ask Joe to coffee? Ugh. My report is due tomorrow."

We're all busy.

But if you get into the habit of "connecting" at the same time on the same day each week, it becomes easier.

Then it becomes a habit.

Pro Tip: Create recurring calendar holds. When we advise executives on utilizing LinkedIn, their biggest hurdle is always "finding the time to do it." We add "meetings" on their calendars. A thirty-minute block once a week for them to focus and complete the task. Guess what? They find the time.

Pro Tip: Add someone's work anniversary or birthday to your calendar. Sending a quick "Happy birthday—coffee soon?" text is easy.

SECTION 9

SCRIPTS, TEMPLATES AND EXAMPLES

Practical, usable, modern templates.

45
Reaching Out to People You Already Know

You can customize these, but the structure stays the same.

Option 1:

"Hi [Name], you crossed my mind and I wanted to say hello. How are things?"

Option 2:

"Hi [Name], I saw this and thought of you. Hope you're doing well.

[Insert link to article, video or picture]"

Option 3:

"Hi [Name]—I'd love to reconnect if you're up for it."

Short. Warm. Real.

When I left my corporate job in 2018, I didn't land my former employer as a client. Everyone asked me, "Did they hire you as a consultant?" No. But I left there with hundreds of connections. After a few months, I started intentionally reaching out to folks to catch up.

"Hey! How are things going? Want to catch up over a coffee? My treat." I wanted them to know what I was working on, that I was open to new clients. But I also wanted to hear about how their work was going, the challenges they were facing. My goal of these meetings wasn't to land new business. It was for them to know how my professional work was going. I also genuinely cared about them and wanted to know about their work, their family, their life. Maybe they were looking to change jobs and I could help connect them with people I knew.

These meetings didn't immediately yield results. Nor did I expect them to. But they strengthened the relationships. And that was the point. The tap.

The investment. And if they were talking to someone who said, "I need help with [insert relevant communications topic here]," my connection might just say, "You should call Katie."

And after a few months, the calls started coming in.

46
Following Up

❜

Use after a meeting, introduction, or conversation:

"Thank you again for your time today. It means a lot to me . . . I know how busy you are.

I took away a lot from what you shared about [topic]. Grateful for the conversation."

If they haven't responded to a request:

"Hi [Name], pinging this to the top in case it got buried. No rush."

Professional. Nonintrusive.

47
Making an Introduction

"Adding you both here—I think you'll enjoy connecting.

[Name 1], meet [Name 2].

Reason for intro: [Insert].

I'll let you two take it from here."

Pro Tip: Keep your reason short.

48
Asking for Advice

"Do you have fifteen minutes sometime this month? I'd value your perspective on something I'm exploring. I pasted my avails below."

People say yes to this.

49
Asking to Meet

"Would you be open to grabbing a coffee (or quick video chat) sometime in the next few weeks? I'd love to catch up. I pasted my avails below."

Clear. Friendly. Easy to accept.

50
Forgot Their Name

"Hi there. I'm Katie. I know we've met, but your name just escaped me. Remind me?"

This line saves everyone.

Pro Tip: Add a note in your contacts or Notes-type app so you remember next time.

51
Ending the Conversation

At a networking event:

"Great chatting with you. I'll let you mingle. Hope to see you again soon."

During coffee:

"This has been so valuable. Thank you so much for your time."

Or on Zoom:

"Looks like we covered everything—thanks again for your time."

52
If You Tend to Come on Too Strong

If you tend to lead with enthusiasm, energy, big ideas—slow down.

People need space to talk.

Try this:

- Ask more questions than you answer.
- Let them lead the conversation.
- Match their tone.
- Share less, listen more.

You don't need to be the star.

You need to be the connector.

You don't need to be the star.

You need to be the connector.

Everyone tells me how nice my mom is. As her daughter, especially during typical teenage years, "nice" wasn't the adjective I used to describe her. But, man, she is kind and generous. It took me years to see why everyone who met her instantly adored her. And then I realized. She listens. She looks you in the eye, she smiles. She asks questions. And more questions. She makes everyone feel like they're the most important person, the only person in the room. Like she has nowhere to be but there talking to you. Listening creates connection.

Pro Tip: Finding yourself talking too much? Take a breath and say, "You know, I tend to talk too much. I'd be remiss if I didn't ask about you."

53
If You're Introverted

Introversion is not a disadvantage.

It's an advantage. Introverts listen, observe and ask thoughtful questions.

Here's your strategy:

- Prepare three to five questions in advance.
- Script your intro.
- Use "Tell me more about . . ."
- Give yourself permission to pause.
- Don't try to be extroverted. Just be curious.

Curiosity builds more trust than charisma.

Pro Tip: Feeling uncomfortable with silence? Don't. It's natural. Use the moment to say, "You know,

Curiosity builds more trust than charisma.

I pulled together a few questions for you before today's meeting. Do you mind if I look at my list real quick?" I love following up someone's answer with, "Tell me more about that . . ." or "That's so interesting. Can you dig in a bit more?" or "I love that. Do you have any other stories like that?"

CONCLUSION: TAKE THIS WITH YOU

Networking isn't about being impressive.

It's about being curious.

It's not about chasing opportunities.

It's about nurturing relationships.

It's not about self-promotion.

It's about shared momentum.

It's about helping others connect and succeed in their professional lives.

Maintaining relationships of all kinds with intention and sincerity.

Because helping others is helping you.

Because we all rise together.

Every job you'll ever get, every project you'll lead, every door that opens in your life . . . it won't happen because you mastered a perfect script or showed up at the right event.

It will happen because people know you.

People trust you.

People remember you.

People want to help you succeed.

People want you to help others succeed.

But you need to build up your savings account **before you actually need it.**

The work starts now.

You love your job? I love to hear it!

Start making deposits now, and you'll have equity built up in case your feelings about your job change in a year or two.

This book gave you the steps.

The stories you insert will make it yours.

The practice you put into relationships will make it happen.

Start small.

Build consistently.

Show up.

Listen.

Follow up.

And never forget:

Real networking is human.

And you already know everyone you need.

ENDNOTES

1. Jasmine Escalera, "Networking Nation: 54% of Workers Got Hired Through a Connection," *My Perfect Resume*, August 12, 2025, https://www.myperfectresume.com/career-center/careers/basics/networking-nation.
2. LinkedIn Corporate Communications, "Eighty-Percent of Professionals Consider Networking Important to Career Success," *LinkedIn Pressroom*, June 22, 2017, https://news.linkedin.com/2017/6/eighty-percent-of-professionals-consider-networking-important-to-career-success.
3. Josh Howarth, "22+ Referral Marketing Statistics (New For 2024)," *Exploding Topics*, November 14, 2023, https://explodingtopics.com/blog/referral-marketing-stats.
4. David G. Wiczer, "Jobs Found Through Referrals Pay More," *Federal Reserve Bank of St. Louis,*

On The Economy Blog, July 19, 2016, https://www.stlouisfed.org/on-the-economy/2016/july/jobs-found-referrals-pay-more.

5. The Kevin Bacon Effect is an adaptation on the Six Degrees of Separation, a theory that any two people are connected through a social chain of no more than six acquaintances. Just as you can connect any actor to 80s heartthrob actor Kevin Bacon in no more than six movies.

ACKNOWLEDGEMENTS

You know who you are.

ABOUT THE AUTHOR

Katie Regan is the founder and CEO of Kirkpatrick Group, a strategic and integrated communications firm. Her path to entrepreneurship began as a side hustle when she started Comma Girl, today known as Kirkpatrick Group, after college. The demand for her writing, strategy, counsel and communications expertise steadily increased until she decided to run the business full time and leave her corporate job in early 2018. Today, she and her fully remote team primarily support B2B clients in manufacturing, industrial, R&D, health care and education. One hundred percent of new business is generated through intentional networking and referrals. www.kirkpat.com

As an undergraduate at Robert Morris University (Moon Township, Pennsylvania), Katie played NCAA Division I soccer and graduated with BAs in English and communications in 2008. She earned her MBA from the University of Pittsburgh Joseph M. Katz Graduate School of Business in 2013. Throughout her career, she has always prioritized supporting and mentoring the next generation of communicators, women leaders and student athletes.

She credits her professional success on her ability to network, a skill she unknowingly began as an adolescent in neighborhood family kitchens across Johnstown, Pennsylvania, and her belief that **a rising tide lifts all boats**.

kirkpat.com | LinkedIn: @katiekregan | Instagram: @katiekregan

www.ingramcontent.com/pod-product-compliance
Lightning Source LLC
LaVergne TN
LVHW091312150826
845673LV00006B/1621

* 9 7 9 8 8 8 7 9 7 2 4 7 3 *